Advance Praise for *Rending the Garment*

In one memorable episode in Willa Schneberg's Rending the Garment, the author's dying mother sits by the hospital bed of the Israeli poet Abba Kovner. "Stars don't go out when we die," he writes on her notepad. "Now you're talking," she writes in reply. This funny, poignant imagined moment is representative of the moments Schneberg has gathered to create her richly woven memoir in poetry of a loving, contentious Jewish family and the world they lived in of junk men, corset shops, and immigrant ambitions.

Lee Sharkey,
author of *Calendars of Fire* & editor of the Beloit Poetry Journal.

In Rending the Garment Willa Schneberg juxtaposes humor and heart-break, Jewish Brooklyn's cultural/ linguistic referents and post-modernity. Readers hear the iconic, self-mocking conversation of familial bickering and the deep devotion of a daughter charged with helping her parents die "good" deaths. "Soon it will be as if language never knew him," says one speaker of her father. With precise, unsparing detail, Schneberg's language rewards our journey into the difficult, mortal territory we all share.

Robin Becker, author of *Tiger Heron*

Advance Praise for *Rending the Garment*

Rending the Garment tells a familiar tale, the Jewish immigrant family romance, but with an important difference: using shifting points of views and narrative interruptions (biographical essays, scolding notes from school Principals, diary entries), not to mention a cast of characters as lively as a borscht belt revue, Willa Schneberg tells her story from the inside, where grief and love live side by side in bed, "neither old, nor young" bodies outside of time. A fresh, original and moving addition to our literature.

Philip Schultz, Pulitzer Prize winner for *Failure* (poems)

Rending the Garment draws us intimately into one family—and through them into the world of immigrant Jews born almost a century ago and their lives in America. Willa Schneberg has a fine ear and her poems capture their voices, their cadences, the way they think, mixing Yiddish with English, the old and the new. The people of her poems come alive on the page: irreverent, beautiful, flawed, funny, sad, loving, opinionated, stubborn, real. They embody a wealth of contradictions, perfectly exemplified in these lines that her mother–who smoked so glamorously and lost her voice to cancer–writes in a notebook near the end of her life, "I'm Jewish./There is no God." I recognize these people and I come to care for them deeply.

Ellen Bass, author of *Like a Beggar* (forthcoming)
and *The Human Line*

Rending the Garment

Distributed by: Ingram Periodicals Inc.,18 Ingram Blvd., LaVergne,
TN 37086 and Ubiquity Distributors, Inc. 607 Degraw St.,
Brooklyn, NY 11217 and Small Press Distribution, 1341 Seventh St.,
Berkeley, CA 94710. Available also from Box Turtle Press.
ISBN: 978-1-893654-14-3

Cover photos provided by Willa Schneberg
Book design: Anne Lawrence
Typeset in Garamond and Futura Book

Copyright © 2014 Willa Schneberg
Publisher: Box Turtle Press
184 Franklin Street, New York, NY 10013
212.219.9278; mudfishmag@aol.com
www.mudfish.org

MUDFISH INDIVIDUAL POET SERIES # 8

Rending the Garment

by

Willa Schneberg

ACKNOWLEDGMENTS

I am grateful to so many who were part of this book, particularly Frances Payne Adler, John Morrison and Barry Sanders for their inspired editorial acumen; my poetry critique groups "The Odds" and "The Pearls;" Fred Marchant, David Zimmerman, Margaret and Doug Stow; Jill Hoffman, my publisher, who said "the poems made her nose run;" Anne Lawrence for her superb cover designs; and Jack Herz and Deborah Jayne for helping me get *Rending the Garment* into the hands of readers.

I would like to thank the following publications and anthologies where work has appeared:

americas review: "Someone I Don't Know Is Being Murdered"

The Barefoot Review: "At The Seaview Nursing Home," new title "At The Oceanside Nursing Home," "The Spoon," "Removing the Intravenous Line"(different version), "Phone Calls, 3 AM," "Hospice"

Bridges: A Jewish Feminist Journal: "In an Airplane Lavatory on Route to Her New Home," "On A Good Morning" (different version), "My Hair," "Hunger Strike" (different version), "Piercing One Ear"

Drash: A Northwest Mosaic: "Not My Type," "The Blackout"

The Grove Review: "Once He Owned Language"

In the Margins of the World, Plain View Press: "A Tunnel Like Any Other" (different version), new title "Tunnel Vision"

Jefferson Monthly: "Ben's Shoes"

Muddy River Poetry Review: "Junk Men"

Nervy Girl: "Willa's Kapparot" (different version)

The Oregonian: "Laryngectomy"

The Portland Alliance: "Teaching Poetry At The Postgraduate Center for Mental Health" (different version)

Portland Review: "Post-Its," "Live Incubator Baby Only 25 Cents!," "Ben Schneberg Writes to Emily Dickinson"

Storytelling in Cambodia, Calyx Books: "Ben's Shoes," "Laryngectomy," "Grief"

21st Century Text: "Bicycling in Belize"

Windfall: A Journal of Poetry of Place: "Ode to Rothko"

Women's Review of Books: "Rending the Garment," "Smoking Raleighs"

Writers' Dojo: "Her Life as a Reader" (different version)

ANTHOLOGIES & LIMITED EDITION LETTERPRESS CHAPBOOK:

The Best Fantasy and Horror Anthology 2006 (St. Martin's Press): "Grief"

Chance of a Ghost (Helicon Nine Editions): "Grief"

Knocking at the Door: Approaching the Other (Birch Bench Press): "Taking Sides" (different version)

Voices Israel Anthologies, 2007, 2010, 2012 (Voices Israel Group of Poets in English): "Smoking Raleighs," "Penmanship," "Esther Schneberg Visits Abba Kovner," "Swank," "King Bowl of Brooklyn"

Walking Bridges Using Poetry as a Compass (Urban Adventure Press): "Piercing One Ear"

The Books of Esther (Paper Crane Press): "In an Airplane Lavatory on Route to Her New Home," "Laryngectomy," "Swank," "A Good Time to Die,"(new title "Bin Laden's Body)," "Rending the Garment." Produced in conjunction with the exhibit of the same name, Oregon Jewish Museum, September - November 2012

Also by Willa Schneberg:

Box Poems
In The Margins of the World
Storytelling in Cambodia
The Books of Esther

CONTENTS

*For Esther and Ben who will not just disappear "into that good night,"
and to my husband Robin for his superb editing skills, and his strong belief
in my work, which has never faltered.*

SECTION ONE

BEN, ESTHER & WILLA

BEN, ESTHER & WILLA

FIRE

Esther Schneberg Wins Essay Prize, 1931

I stood on the steps of City Hall
waiting for the big muckamucks,
fidgeting with the clasp of the new purse
my mother bought for the occasion,
or waving a small American flag.

The First Prize winner of the
"Fire Prevention in the Home" Essay Contest,
a wheelchair-bound girl, arrived
in a fire truck sirens blazing.
It must have been a big deal for my parents,
or they wouldn't have saved the clipping of
461 Model Pupils Honored for Fire Prevention.

How could I care when I was eleven
that people kept gasoline, benzene and naphtha
in their homes. We didn't,
or that a fire escape was a fire exit,
not a place for rags, brooms or mops. Ours wasn't.
I just wanted an "A."

I knew what I couldn't write about:
boys in the dumb classes
bludgeoning squirrels to death,
lighting matches underneath swing sets,
then running across the street to watch
poles melt and wooden seats become charred nothings.

But now since I'm good as dead
I know anger – the kind

that makes you want to hurl yourself
off a tall building, or fill the tub
with water and drop in the hairdryer,
I understand the draw of a can of gasoline
and a match in the moonlight, the boom,
the hiss of cold flames.

THE LAST SON

Wolf has no time to grieve his Leah.
He must find another mother quick
for Abraham, Sarah, David, Rose and Bess,
and get back to the store.

Soon after sitting shiva
Wolf brings a blue-eyed blonde into the house,
a "Jewish shiksa," and her daughter
who will sleep in the living room on a Murphy bed.
None of the kids want her in their rooms.

The new wife makes Shabbos.
The boys don't shower or wear fresh shirts.
The girls refuse to light candles or say the *brucha*
beckoning the Shekinah to dwell behind their eyes.

When Wolf enters her
she won't give him her lips.
Ben is conceived.

Esther D. Schneberg   5/28/86
English

MY TWO GRANDMOTHERS

Until I was ten, I knew only one grandmother, my father's mother. I called her "Baba." She looked like no other grandmother on my block. She did not have the capacious lap that grandmas are supposed to have. She was too slender and slight. She wore dark clothes and on her head a black lace scarf that fell in folds on each side of her face to mid-skirt. Startling in contrast to her somber lace were her pale, oval face and her light blue eyes like a halcyon sky. Her hair, which she uncovered only when going to bed, was smooth and black, caught in a bun.

My mother insisted that Grandma do no chores and that her visit was to be a complete vacation. They spent many hours in Yiddish conversation, when Baba was not reading her Bible and observing the daily prayers. I cannot forget my mother's awe and respect as she sat opposite Baba in the dining room. Baba, Bible in hand was ensconced in our high-backed, rococo framed red velvet armchair. As they spoke, the soft light from partially open Venetian blinds encircled them. I wanted to be in that aura, so I memorized the *Modeh Ani*, the short prayer on arising in praise of God for surviving sleep's small death. My reward was Baba's embrace and her delight in me.

My other grandmother, my mother's mother, whom I shall call Baba Reizel, I did not meet until I was 10. She was lying in bed obviously very ill, in a white cotton lace-trimmed nightgown. Hovering around her bed were my grandfather, her children in the States and all the grandchildren newly introduced to her. Beside her bed was a wig. She said, "You see this *sheitel*, I will never wear it again. I don't have to, I am in America." My eyes moved to her brown slightly grey hair worn in ringlets close to her head. With her sloe eyes and her high cheekbones, she looked like a pixie. She was 59. Awaiting her was a completely furnished apartment, which she never saw.

MAMIE DANENHIRSCH VISITS HAZEL HALL

Poet and seamstress, Hazel Hall (1886-1924), lived in Portland, Oregon.

> *Sorrow's thread is a long thread.*
> Hazel Hall

Hazel has many wealthy customers
desiring wedding crinolines
and monograms on their napkins.
My grandma, Mamie wants to
meet with her to discuss business.

Climbing up the stairs to Hazel's bedroom,
she thinks of names for her store:
Mamie's Custom Corsets,
Custom-made by Mamie.

It is late April, but cold.
The mirror on the sill gives Hazel
a better view, hail pellets melt in the sun,
Deodar branches droop.

She hears my grandma
on the steps and reluctantly
turns from the window.
She offers her the rocker
and rolls her wheelchair closer.
They touch hands, speak

the language of cross-stitch,
coarse thread, crepe de Chine,
mending, easing and give.

Hazel whispers, "I'm dying.
I will never lie with a man.
Words sown on vellum are becoming my thread.
My strophes hold the cool thin fingers
of those I long to know."

Hazel unravels her soul, and Mamie
who keeps her emotions buttoned-up,
not knowing what to say
hands her the doily
she crocheted as a gift.

Mamie thought they were both practical,
making tangible things with purpose.
She didn't know Hazel was a poet.

My grandma, who puts pen to paper
for shopping lists,
understands the thing itself:
the thimble, the pin cushion; wetting
a polished black thread in her mouth,
its point piercing a needle's eye.

Mamie thinks she shouldn't have come,
that Hazel sees her ambitions as small:

a gold-stenciled Singer
treadle machine in a shoppe,
a bell at its entrance

ringing just often enough.

Hazel says she must rest,
and won't meet Mamie's eyes.

My grandma knows she has overstayed
her welcome. As she flees down the staircase,
she comforts herself:
...so customers have privacy
I'll have three dressing rooms
with curtains for doors.

NOT MY TYPE

Shelly Winters was raised in the Brownsville Section of Brooklyn.

Before the studio made her change her name, her name was Shirley. Her father Jonas Shrift was a tailor cutter, her mother Rose played piano for silent pictures. I can barely recall her sister Blanche. Shirley lived around the corner from me on Berriman. I used to see the family strolling after dinner on Shabbos. As a teenager, Shirley still had baby fat and a big *tuchas*. She was a few years younger than me, so I never saw her around Thomas Jefferson. I'm not sure she even graduated. A lot of the guys I palled around with wanted to get into her pants, but I never went for the slutty type— the peroxide blonde with thick make-up. I like a woman with class, like your mother, who has a brain and isn't running into the bathroom to touch-up her face. I heard somewhere that Shirley and Marilyn Monroe were room-mates in Hollywood. Shirley was divorced three times and was always being *shtupped* by someone (weren't they all?). She even had a dalliance with Clark Gable. I can't believe that an actor of his caliber was interested in her. As for her movies, she played the used and abused waitress, or a jilted factory girl who wound-up dead.

Your mother and I were watching Johnny Carson. Shirley was a guest. *Mittendrinen* she leaves the set, returns with a champagne bucket filled with ice and water, and then proceeds to dump the contents of the bucket over the head of an English actor she dislikes for some cockamamy reason. Your mother says it was because he was a male chauvinist pig. Anyway, the actor tries to attack her...Johnny's crew inter-venes. After the commercial break they are gone. Shirley never learned the mean-ing of refinement. A prank in very poor taste.

I have to hand it to her, when she was too fat and too old to play floozies, she did give a superb performance as the obnoxious, loud-mouthed mother of Anne Frank's love interest. When she donated her Oscar to the Anne Frank Museum, she redeemed herself in my eyes.

SWANK

Once my mother drank New York,
but never more than two Jack Daniels and Coke.
She wore dark red lipstick, her hair in an upsweep
like Tallulah Bankhead to show off her high cheekbones.

On the dentist's arm she floated into Cafe Society Uptown,
and the Cotton Club bewitched
by Lena Horne, Lester Young, Art Tatum,
and Cab Calloway or stomped at the Savoy,
the dazzle nearly getting her into compromising positions.

But no matter what kind of smooching
had been going on, her date would escort her
to her door by 4 AM, when her papa
already dressed and ready
shooed the young man away
before delivering milk to stoops and porches,
sunlight glinting off the squat bottles.

HELL NO!

With a high score on the Civil Service exam,
I landed an appointment as a Tunnel Officer
at an annual salary of $1,800.
Incredible money for 1941
when all the men
except me were overseas.

My mother and my sister Ethel
were so proud.
But I just couldn't
patrol on Holland Tunnel's
railed narrow platform
93 ft. below the Hudson River,
marrying lower Manhattan to Jersey City.

I was supposed to keep moving
except for time to micturate,
wolf down a cold steak sandwich or
a salami on rye.

It felt like cars from both lanes
of traffic were coming at me;
headlights blinding,
I choked on exhaust fumes.

There were supposed to be ducts
to draw in fresh air and
suck out carbon monoxide,

42 blowing fans and 42 exhaust fans,
but the sweat poured through my uniform
and I couldn't stop puking.

I wasn't willing to get buried down there
like the thirteen "sandhogs,"
just regular guys,
who helped to build the damn thing.

FROM ESTHER'S DIARY

Thurs, April 8, 1943, Fort Benning, Georgia

We're still interned in this concentration camp, a ramshackle, former CCC site. We might as well have barbed wire with all the freedoms we have. 105 WAACS huddled together in berths a few inches apart. We use one latrine, and if you're aggressive enough, you can manage what a gentile oaf termed a "bird bath" and what we call a "spit" bath.

Ruby in a bunk on the lower left from me is a tall friendly gal with an expansive nature. She speaks constantly of her lover Red and his way with women. She endorses Northern boys as the best lovers because they are blunt. I like listening to the girls. I'm learning a new language. "Bubbles" means water fountain, people can be as "ugly as a mud fence," and if you worry, "You're missing your pot." My favorite: "I feel like a child without a mommy & daddy at a family reunion."

Last night to lift our morale they imported a band of colored soldiers who played hot music and sang Negro spirituals. Some of them were handsome and built superbly as only Negro men can be.

Today, I was told I'm a sergeant. I'm quite overcome. This ascent in rank has already cost me some potential friends. One of the gals was kind (?) enough to suggest that I take my position seriously and exercise my authority over my inferiors. Is she kidding??

SMOKING RALEIGHS

When my mother still believed
my father was who she wished he was,
she kept a card file of recipes, and
Red Skelton was the voice of Raleigh
whose ads depicted a couple in evening dress—
a man in tails, a woman in a formfitting gown
with a flounce in the back— dancing
as if they owned the hall.

They could have been my parents.
At family affairs distant relatives
asked if they were on the stage,
and my parents flattered and tired
would shake their heads, no,
as they left the floor to look for their table.

My mother would sit down demurely;
my father would sit backward
nonchalantly on a folding chair,
from the inside of his tux jacket
take out the pack, Sir Walter Raleigh
prim on the cover, pat the bottom just enough
for two cigarettes to spring up like skyscrapers,
then pluck a match from the matchbook
of Howard's bar mitzvah,
or Mollie and Irving's wedding,
to light the smokes in his mouth and slowly
place one between my mother's full lips.

LIVE INCUBATOR BABY ONLY 25 CENTS!

Coney Island, 1903-1945

If I slid into this world a few years earlier,
the midway next to Violetta the Armless Wonder,
Princess Wee Wee and
Ajax, the Sword-Swallower,
might have been my only hope.

There were hundreds of naked newborns,
wailing too soon, saved
from Columbia Presbyterian and
St. Claire's, venerable institutions
who weren't sure about Dr. Couney's newfangled
metal and glass womb.
Hospitals wouldn't risk investing in a device
similar to one that hatches chicks,
even though their preemies were dying.

Frantic parents didn't care
that their bald, closed eyed progeny
were part of a freak show,
because now they could grow old.

Paying customers oohed and aahed:
look, a foot the size of a fingernail,
a heart smaller than the gold one
my wife wears around her neck.

MAHJONG INTERLUDE

Boulevard Housing Project, Brooklyn, 1952

The clicking of shuffling tiles
is like sparrows' silvery trills,
the Chinese say, and what I hear is
kibitzing and squawk:
Clark Gable can put his head on my pillow.
How much gelt does your husband dole out?

I won't divulge that I have a B.A. and
don't care about mastering the game,
that these mahjong afternoons
are just an interlude. Soon
I'll make my own money again.

If you don't compete, the women say,
you won't progress past a Chicken Hand.

I'd be happy just rubbing my fingers
across Rivkah's set of cow bone tiles,
butter-popcorn yellow, smooth as piano keys,
her family brought from the Orient;
hand carved with dragons, ladies of the court
and old men in tattered garments with walking sticks
climbing impossibly steep peaks.

We never discuss why her family were stateless
in Shanghai, but we talk about that marvel, Israel,
its pomegranates bursting with billions of seeds,
and that we hope to all be there "next year."
For the other new mothers it is the only reason to leave

America, but I also want to travel to countries
that don't exist because of gas chambers.

In each other's apartments with the same layouts and
hospital green walls (for white one pays extra), we sing
the praises of Fritchie's and Weinstein's
bungalow colonies where baby bats hang from rafters,
and we with fingers purple from huckleberry picking
capture fireflies in mason jars.

Soon we are arguing:
who gives a better performance,
Shecky Green or Henny Youngman.
In the timeless two hours before
our husbands come home,
I almost fit in.

THE ROSE CORSET SHOPPE

Everywhere boxes are filled with Maidenforms
the size of clown noses,
single scoops of ice-cream,
Pensy Pinky rubber balls,
Aunt Ethel's round throw pillows, and
Dale Evans' saddlebags.

Some feel stiff when I poke them,
others are soft and flimsy,
a few have padding inside and stand up
on their own like mommy's.
My grandma says some are special,
for women who once had breasts
and gave them away.
I would never do that.

My grandma couldn't be bothered
to change the store's name,
so although she is Mamie, it remains
The Rose Corset Shoppe
with no red roses or a Rose.

Each dressing room doesn't reach the floor,
perfect for me to crawl inside.
The ladies without clothes don't mind
and it's grandma's store.

Me, I only have a chest.
It will be forever
before I get a training bra.

THE JUNK MEN

I can almost hear far off
a faint neighing and clopping,
wagons rattling,
a tinkle of bells
where the farms used to be,
when cows were milked by hand,
and cream topped tin pails.

Although I can't quite make out
your cries for schmattes,
I know what you were saying:
What you don't want I want,
old, too big, too small, broke.
I'm certain you carted away
radios with big dials stuck on one station
and toasters whose coils lost their glow,
but you never came to our door.

You have already vanished
into my dreams and my mother's
tales of her old neighborhood.

You wore gloves without fingers.
Soft knitted monkeys disappeared
inside your overcoats.
You did your shpiels,
sharpened knives, and took away
what was no longer loved.

Now you dwell in the land of the icebox
and the washboard, and I live in a tall building
that thrusts into the sky
with its elevators and incinerator chutes
for throwing away whatever we tire of.

From Ben's papers

BOARD OF EDUCATION OF THE CITY OF NEW YORK

Office of the Principal

Feb. 2, 1959

Dear Mr. Schneberg,

It is to be regretted that your plan book was not completed for the week. Indeed, there were no (lesson) plans at all.

I wish to remind you that the writing of plans, one week in advance, is mandatory for all teachers.

Cordially,

Jacob Landers, Principal

BE CREATIVE

The students will learn soon enough
what I know, that no one will give you a break,
that good looks get you only so far,
that you must succeed because your father failed.

When I was in 9th grade I was the editor
of the *Liberty Bell,* the student newspaper,
Vice-President of the class, a member
of the Latin Club, on the Honor Roll.

Kids nowadays just want to doodle,
look down girls' shirts and get answers
by glancing at their neighbors' tests.

If only Landers could understand,
I have nothing to teach them.

When I tell him they cheat and plagiarize
he mocks me, *Have them write
about* "Plagiarism: What it is, and How to
Recognize and Avoid it." *Be creative.*

He leaves lesson plan ideas in my box,
as if, like a lousy actor, reading more and more
scripts would make me John Barrymore.

AT A KOSHER DELI

Sleepwalking…
on each table I place small bowls filled with brine;
half-sour tomatoes and half-sour pickles
huddle with sour dills.

How long will I keep secret
that I'm a waiter at Grabstein's
serving overstuffed pastrami on seeded-rye
to yokels who never read O'Neill?

I leave home with my leather briefcase
heavy with want ads,
and head to the library
until it's time for my shift to start.

I couldn't stand it anymore,
mere infants daring me to grab their attention
so they might for a second quit
writing on their hands, cracking gum,
throwing spitballs, flatulating loudly.

The last straw was
when Sandy Edelman
begged me to send him to the principal,
to get out of *the most boring
class he ever slept through.*
Every single student snickered.

Now I consolidate ketchup,
balance the lip of a one-third full bottle
on the lip of a half-full bottle and watch
red seep into red glop.

BEN SCHNEBERG MEETS JACOB LAWRENCE AT HILLSIDE HOSPITAL

They walked among the other ghosts, shoulders hunched, heads down. There must have been an instant when the Negro and the Jew locked eyes and read each other's despair.

Was my father a sad man "In The Garden" Lawrence captured in tempera, weeding amidst swirling blossoms of larkspur blue, rose, country kitchen yellow and the green of the newly leafed,

or was he one of the androgynous in "Sedation," dressed in beige and brown-checked pajamas and bathrobes slackly sashed, staring into a bin displaying psychotropic capsules of dazzling oranges, reds and purples?

Did they listen together to classical music on WQXR, the only station my father said was worth a damn. Did my father, who spoke Yiddish like he just got off the boat, teach Lawrence "Oyfn Pripetchik?"

Perhaps Jacob teased Ben that his use of primary colors and flattened simple shapes in the acrylic he labored over in OT might have been influenced by someone he knew.

But they wouldn't talk about why they felt colorless, or of their young wives worried sick at home, only Dr. Klein was privy to that.

When they were discharged, Lawrence had a one-man show at the Downtown Gallery. Aline R. Louchman for the New York Times wrote, "An artist reports on the troubled mind. Jacob Lawrence paints mental moods that startle—as did Van Gogh." My father's hospital stay didn't make the papers, but for a few weeks before discharge Ben held light in the bristles of his brush.

We all know Jacob Lawrence died famous. Children are brought on school busses to see his "Migration Series."

As for Ben Schneberg, his single work of accordion brownstones leaning toward their reflection in a gas lamp-lit pond hangs on my bathroom wall.

PENMANSHIP

I cannot make Esther want another child
or prevent the throbbing in my chest
when I know something terrible will happen
if I go a step further,

but at least I can get this right.
I am not my father,
Wolf, the haberdasher,
who sold tie tacks and silk shirts
to young men with a future,
until he ran away
from bill collectors.

I do not slouch when I ready myself
at the small desk for paying bills,
my feet flat on the floor,
the Waterman still in its case,
vellum sheets slanted to the left.

I'm up to Lesson 26 in my workbook:
The Complete Program for a Better Cursive Handwriting.
I like tracing the *a* sashaying to the *h*,
dipping to the *y* and rising to little hillocks of *m*'s
docilely chained together.
I have perfected my entrance and exit serifs,
my curlicues and the loops of my *p*'s.
Please pare a pair of pears.

Before, I wrote a chicken scrawl,
like someone who could barely sign his name,
a nobody,
not the handsome hand
of a man who leaves shopping lists
for lesser mortals,
who pens words
you do not turn away from.

Tonight's exercise is a formula poem.
I am to trace:
Nothing is...
and add my thoughts with a flourish:
...like a job well done.
Friendship is...
...knowing you won't be let down.

FLIGHT PATH

My parents wait for relatives
to get off 707s.
One crashed in Jamaica Bay.
They wouldn't let me go see it.
Everyone died.

They make me be a member
of the welcoming committee.
I get a few minutes to scan
the boards for departures.
The names roll around my tongue
like m&m's: Luxembourg,
Seoul, Papeete, Quito.

I want outta here—
past the Canarsie Pier,
Long Island Sound,
and the humongous Atlantic.

Back home, I adjust the rabbit-ears
on top of the TV. The ordeal
of *tantes* Millie and Mollie pinching me,
plying me with hard candies,
and telling me to be good
is finally over.

So close to Idlewild,
airplanes mess with the reception,
and leave
without me.

KING BOWL OF BROOKLYN

We take off our everyday shoes
and put on new red leather lace-ups
with a chartreuse stripe down the middle.
Since I'm girly, my ball must be light
with holes that don't swallow my fingers,
and purple (there aren't pink ones).

Rhonda likes the feel of the fat pencils,
so she keeps score. Faye spreads out our stash
of Juicy Fruit gum, red licorice,
pink Sno Balls, Twinkies and Pepsi in bottles
on the Formica table top
decorated with "B" for Brunswick,
and pins floating in air.

Everywhere polished alleys gleam,
pins crash, people cheer, contraptions
drag away pins and place them back
perfectly, unless they don't—
then the pin boys have to do it by hand.
There is one I like. I won't tell
Rhonda or Faye. They might like him too.

When it's my turn,
everyone disappears.
I love that moment.
Centering myself in front of the middle pin,
I pull my arm back and release— no power.

My body sways to the right
to keep it from being a gutter ball.
The ball creeps so slowly
I walk back to my seat defeated,
then turn around to discover
I'm a princess: the pins
fall on their faces
before me.

THE BLACKOUT

Nov. 9, 1965

Heinz Vegetarian beans in the can
sit in a pot of boiling water.
In the steamer, a chunk of frozen
broccoli separates into little trees.

On aluminum foil
lamb chop fat glistens,
tries to burst into flame,
but never does.

I put the Cokes on the table.
My father clanks out the metal ice
tray's ice into a bowl. I'm not allowed
to pick up a cube. I like how it stings
and sticks to my fingers. How soon
will I be excused?

The bottle cap leaps
off— no hiss of air, no fizz.
Then the screaming begins. My father:
The one time you actually go to the store,
you get pop with no pep. My mother:
Thanks a lot, this is why I let you do the shopping.
I curl into a ball they cannot see.

I'm thirteen, and training them to knock
before they open the door to my room.
Sometimes I touch myself
down there...
imagining I'm chosen by the Sultan.

What's happening?

The lights are out as far as I can see, and
even past Floyd Bennett Field
where Amelia Earhart and Howard Hughes were cheered,
and beyond Inwood and Lawrence, where grown-ups move
when their kids get too wild.

For once, something different—

if there can be a blackout
in the greatest city in the world,
anything is possible.

We can't find candles,
except for Yahrzeit.

Even my parents are quiet
as we eat and stare
into the pitch.

TAKING SIDES

Ocean Hill-Brownsville, Brooklyn, Nov. 1968

My mother's on the picket line,
freezing, stamping her feet,
walking round and around.
She holds a cup of coffee
in one hand, and in the other
carries the cardboard sign
she made herself:

PROTECT JOBS FOR ALL
THIS IS NOT ABOUT RACE

On the collar of her red cloth coat
she proudly displays her UFT button.
With stinging ears she hears some fellow strikers
call scabs "nigger lovers" as they run
past into my high school.

My mother is sure that the ones inside
want a Jose Fernandez
or a Latitia Washington to succeed
as much as she does.
Her good guys are Albert Shanker,
Bayard Rustin and Martin Luther King.

The teacher I have a crush on
crossed the line. He loved *On the Road*,
lived in Paris, and writes on the top of my poems,
"This is great stuff, man."

His heroes are John Lindsey, Julius Lester and Malcolm X.
Inside with him are some people who call
Jewish teachers "bloodsucking exploiters."
One even taught a black kid to write:
> *Hey, Jew boy, with that yarmulke on your head,*
> *you pale-faced Jew boy,*
> *I wish you were dead.*

I'll never cross a picket line. Never.
My mother would kill me if I did.
I like staying home in my room anyway
rereading *The Diary of Anne Frank*
(at least she got kissed
by Peter Van Daan),
instead of completing the assignment

From Slavery to Freedom: A History of Afro-Americans,
about John Brown. He killed five pro-slavery people,
raided Harpers Ferry to steal guns
for his runaway slave colony.
Emerson and Thoreau praised him.
I think he was a hero, but maybe he wasn't.
I can't say if John Brown was a freedom fighter
or a plain old murderer, but unlike me
he could take sides.

THE SPERM INCIDENT

Thomas Jefferson High School has five stories,
metal detectors and cops everywhere.
The original magnificent marble staircase, now scuffed and worn,
spirals from floor to floor.

Standing on the second landing, something,
I think a small balloon, plops on my head.
A viscous salty substance mats my hair and runs down my face.
I feel mortified like when I took off my suit coat and forgot
I was wearing only a dickey over my bra.

I hear the slap of high-fiving above me.

How could I have believed I am not the enemy?

TUNNEL VISION

Although tunnels never end,
when the young psychologist
he loves like a son
says he'll wait on the other side,
Ben pretends he's a rubber ball
that rolls in by mistake:

sick to his stomach,
gulping air,
his heart pounds
like when he lost his wife
at the behemoth department store
on Herald Square.

But the tunnel doesn't chain him to stone
or cover his eyes with its black palms.
Instead he feels sunlight on his face,
and bellows: *fuck-you all,*
I licked this thing!

EAGLETON, I KNOW HOW YOU FEEL

Thomas Eagleton was the Democratic Vice Presidential Nominee in 1972.
Journalists Clark Hoyt & Robert S. Boyd reported on Eagleton's treatment for depression.

Chocolate syrup and seltzer on our lips,
we would sit in a red-vinyl booth, snarl
and spit at the *momzers* who destroyed our lives,
their punishment: to be permanently strapped
inside our black cloud. Only then would they understand
the joylessness we wear as skin.

You'd rave: John Adams had several nervous breakdowns.
I'd rant: Franklin Pierce was a drunk;
when Rutherford Hayes was young he wandered
the streets weeping.
Yet they all managed to govern.

We would clink to Lincoln and the melancholy
that dripped from him. He was our greatest
president, I'd say, and implore: So why couldn't you serve
on the McGovern ticket? Labor liked you.
You're a decent guy, a family man.

You would shake your head, roll your eyes,
and look into your tumbler, your voice quaking:
Why did those callous bastards think
it was their duty to break the story?

Somehow, being "crazy" before,
you still managed to get elected senator.

They said they did it for the good of the country.

I will never understand how ruining
someone's career merits a Pulitzer.

FALSE ALARM

I never talk sex with you,
you who slept only with my father.
But at seventeen,
going almost all the way
with the head counselor
at Camp Louemma,
I'm scared I'm pregnant,
so I have to.

I leave the campers
to make their plastic lanyards
and slam tennis balls
without my guidance,
since I need yours.

Rod is five years older, not Jewish,
with blonde hair all over his body
even his back. He chose me,
not other cuter junior counselors.

Daddy and you are waiting.
I run off the Trailways bus at Port Authority
heaving with tears into your arms;
you have already arranged
the appointment with a gynecologist
and there is no lecture.

It was a sultry night,
below measles of stars I never see in the City,
on a blanket that hides the prickly groundcover;
small beneath him, fireflies
the only peeping toms,
his tongue deep in my mouth,
my pores open to his touch,
but it's not his fingers pushing aside
the leg hole of my panties,
but something swollen, wet and pulsating.

TEACHING POETRY AT THE POSTGRADUATE CENTER FOR MENTAL HEALTH

Night comes on and the nurses
offer up a pill
while the stars in the sky
burn like neon jacks.

Ann Sexton

I fear I will end up like Ann Sexton,
a patient in the same mental hospital
where she taught poetry to "Mayflower screwballs"
with names like Higginson and Bowditch.

My students subsist in childhood bedrooms,
group homes, flophouses, efficiencies,
having earned their diplomas
from Creedmore, Pilgrim State and Bellevue.

In group they write:
"I hate my finger. It is bent and ugly..."
"Is madness madness?" "... with you, neither female
nor male, simply both..."
"... but one day I was going and I met myself coming,
 so I killed myself."

Sometimes while teaching I see myself
squinched up, facing the wall;

instead of croaking alone,
we O.D. in our poems.

WILLA'S KAPPAROT

This is my substitute, this is my exchange, this is my atonement.

A hen used to accept my sorrow.
I would hold it squawking in my left hand,
press my right on the crest of its head,
swing it three times below the sky and
thank it for taking my torment into its body.
So when I cut the jugular I was happy.
Soon it would be boiling in the cast iron pot
and I would eat morsels off its feet.
Before I knew it, anguish would crawl back in
through the skylight and each keyhole and crack,
weekly, then daily.

I couldn't eat all those chickens.
I gave them to everyone in my building and
to anyone in the street who was willing
to take a carcass off my hands.

When I could not stand the slaughter anymore
I would imagine swinging the hens
over head and no killing,
but setting them down to peck and scratch
once the ground stopped spinning.
When they knew I knew I didn't need them,
they vanished.
Now I dab *tzuris* behind my ears
and persevere.

INTERVIEW WITH MY FATHER

Willa, the truth of the matter is in spite of your questions, I do not choose to answer them at this time. The mere fact that you want an answer does not mean I must give you one. You are interested in cemeteries and death arrangements and I have all that material for you.

Why did you let me set this up and then say that you don't want to be interviewed? Why did you say plug in the tape recorder in this outlet, if you didn't want to?

In regard to cemetery properties, we own four graves in the New Montefiore Cemetery at Pinelawn in Babylon, Long Island. It's the place where Uncle Hymie, Tante Bessie and Irving are buried.

As far as actual funeral arrangements are concerned, I have not made my mind up yet, but I have been seriously considering giving my body to Tisch Hospital. I don't know if they would be interested in anyone of my age; on the other hand it may be of interest to students studying bypass surgery. Another possibility is that I may be cremated.

So then you wouldn't be using the cemetery plot?

If they want to put my remains in an urn that would be interred in the plot, yes. I would like to be close to your mother and you. It does not have to take up an entire grave. If the urn is actually placed where Esther will finally rest that is alright with me too, which means two graves would be available for whoever wants them or needs them. Graves are very, very expensive, you know.

This is the deed showing we own four graves and the descriptions of all of them. It is a reasonably nice cemetery, in spite of the fact that we don't have the most attractive spot. The deed and other related papers are all kept in the filing cabinet, where your mother's papers are, under "C" for cemetery. I hope you'll be around for my funeral.

It is very, very simple. This is what Thomas Mann said, "A man's dying is more the survivors affair than his own."

What do you mean if I'm around?

I don't know how convenient it is to fly in and out of Cambodia.

Obviously, if you die while I'm gone, I'll come home for your funeral.

As far as going into my life, I have an excellent tape recorder myself. One of these days in the not too distant future, I will record myself and send you a copy. Right now I don't feel like getting involved.

That's fine, but I don't expect you to do it on your own. Maybe tomorrow you'll consent to the interview.

SOMEONE I DON'T KNOW IS BEING MURDERED

Lay Sok Phiep and Atsuhito Nakata were ambushed in Kompong Thom Province,
April 8, 1993

I had never personally known anyone who was murdered. My Vietnam War protest days were already over during the "Pol Pot Time." I was living in NYC, throwing Japanese-style tea bowls and was involved with two guys: a Belgian who wrote songs like Jacques Brel, but turned out to be a neo-Nazi, and a macrobiotic who watched French films all day long and had to be forcibly escorted from my apt. by Bill and Jose, two friends from the old neighborhood. While I dreamt of the place on earth farthest away from my parents, I chaperoned people labeled mentally ill to a hippie printer who ran his press in the buff, and would print for nothing the works of groups he felt dealt with their oppression in a pc way. So, overnight a new chapter of Mental Patients Liberation was born. The ink wasn't even dry on the magazines when the administration where I taught the poetry group locked the "subversive pamphlets" in a file cabinet, stating they wouldn't return them until the "chronics" blacked out their last names with magic markers. It was 1976 and I was finding myself. I didn't know or care that maybe two million Khmers were being slaughtered for hiding a page from a book or hoarding kernels of rice.

Almost twenty years later I'm living alone in Phnom Penh, preparations for "free and fair" elections are going on around me, and still no one I know has been murdered. I hear the NADK are executing Vietnamese fisherfolk and prostitutes. NADK and CPAF are doing each other in, and starving soldiers of all factions are using weapons supposedly cantoned to steal *riels* or pig heads from the laps of civilians bicycling home after dark, but I do know Lay Sok and Atsu a little.

Although Atsu is Japanese, his English is probably better than mine, but he doesn't think so. He asks me to proofread the memo he has written to upgrade the salary of his interpreter Lay Sok, who will be shot dead when a bullet from an AK 47 will puncture his stomach, arm and chest. Lay Sok was improving his English by reading *Newsweek* in his office in Prasat Sambo. Atsu who is only twenty-five, soon to be a bridegroom, believes in democracy, a free-market economy, the essential goodness of humankind, and did not excuse Japan's imperialism or the atom bomb, will be shot in the head at close range as he cowers beneath his vehicle, his face in the mud. At first we were sure the NADK had orchestrated it. Atsu was being targeted because he was from that almost western Asian country in its first mission since WW II. But later we will learn the culprit was a Khmer acting alone, pissed he didn't get a transistor radio or a job as a registrar.

Some of my fellow DES's have stopped believing "free and fair" elections are still possible. Tired of having their offices shot up or the tents where election workers sleep hit by rocket-propelled grenades, they will leave. I remain steadfast in my opinion that New York City is more dangerous. It is my job to ensure that the Medical Branch transports Atsu's body from the Field Hospital to the Ounalom Pagoda, the St. Patrick's of Phnom Penh. The smoke from the crematorium chokes the sky and someone I don't know is being murdered.

LONG DAY'S JOURNEY INTO NIGHT AT THE SEAVIEW BRANCH OF THE BROOKLYN PUBLIC LIBRARY

For a second you see...
For a second there is meaning!

Those are Marv's lines, the junior librarian,
the son I never had. I play the patriarch,
James Tyrone Sr., a failed Shakespearean actor,
who went for the bucks rather than greatness

against Marv's tubercular Edmund
who would become Eugene O'Neill,
the master of modern American drama.

Holding the script in my hand,
I'm not here in the conference room
of a backwater branch of the library,
performing for a dozen patrons
who wandered in to browse the shelves.

For once my matinee idol looks have a purpose.
I'm at the Helen Hayes electrifying the audience
with the ferocity of my delivery:

I'd be willing to have no home but the poorhouse
in my old age if I could look back now
on having been the fine artist I might have been.

BEN SCHNEBERG WRITES TO EMILY DICKINSON

And Something's odd—within—
That person that I was—
And this One—do not feel the same—
Could it be Madness—this?

                                                    Emily Dickinson

Emily, I am better now. I feel swell.
Tunnels, bridges and new towns
welcome me.

I will book a train from Grand Central Station
and hire a buggy to your father's house.

If you agree, and I pray you will,
I will visit in a fortnight. A Sunday afternoon?

All I ask is that you open your gate
and extend your hand.

Perhaps in time
when you trust me a little,
you will venture outside,
and we will sit together
in the buggy's cab in front of your house.

When you're ready, with a tickle
of the whip, the horses will trot slowly
and we will see First Church's spire
from the safety of our cab,

or hide behind a maple tree
and listen to the feet go in.

My greatest desire
is to quiet your fear as we go inside.
I know… your breath will quicken,
your heart will race
like a stampede of cattle.

As we stroll through the white doors
with your hand on my arm
the panic will pass like a fever,
and when we sit
in the last pew,
your heart will again tick
benignly as a clock.

BEN CALLS HIS DAUGHTER FROM A HOSPITAL IN BROOKLYN

We've been here only a few hours and already had visitors.

Crown Heights. Some Chabad children and women wearing *sheitel*s
expensive as your mother's mink stole.

Your mother, more power to her, cut their mitzvah short.

She said, We don't believe in the messiah, whether he's Schneerson or Jesus.

Okay, okay...We had just returned from one of your mother's stores.
I needed the bathroom. When I was young and had a few drinks
I could hold it until I found a toilet.

We are fine now.

So, this is what happened: I pressed the button on the gadget
that closes the garage, ran to the small bathroom. Your mother
followed me into the house in her usual slow fashion, the screen door
slammed behind us like always.

We started watching a cop show eating frozen yogurt.

Yeah, okay, I left the car running.

Your mother says Ben, I don't feel right, I can't catch my breath.

She called the ambulance. How is everybody in Portland?

Can you hear me?

I know I'm whispering. I don't want your mother to hear this—
the doctors said an hour longer, it would've been all over.

LATE VISIT

You are eighty-three and must doze.
I tuck a down comforter
around your hands and feet. Later,
when I project slides of Angkor
on a white wall you feign interest.

Dining together at a posh restaurant,
early evening, your attention is riveted
on a pork chop your doctor
forbade you to eat:
This cut is better than anything
I ever had in New York.

We will stand in my backyard
under a budding magnolia,
beneath sky the color of dark blue veins,
your shoulder brushing mine,
not talking, remembering
that when I was little
we were close:

At Jones Beach I would leap
into cold, crashing spume,
as you waited on shore with two large towels—
one for wrapping me up, patting me dry,
and the other for me to sprawl on.
Eyes closed, sun enveloping us,
a transistor radio between our bodies—
we would rock to the music.

AT THE OCEANSIDE NURSING HOME

The attendant spies the daughter walking down the hall,
and sucks on every last illicit second of telephone time
to gab with her friend about their girlhoods
in Barbados. When the daughter enters the room
she hangs up.

The daughter barely listens to the attendant *kvetch*
how rudely the nurses and aides treat her.
The daughter understands their outrage:
she gets paid three or four times more
for diapering one old baby
than they make removing bed pans
from underneath seventy-five behinds.

But the daughter won't fire her.
She needs to pretend
this paid helper keeps one father alive,
and that his brain
like dried porcini mushrooms
soaking in cold water,
will spring back to life.

THE SPOON

Every holiday with a diamond cutter's precision
he carved plump juicy birds;
white meat left side of platter, dark on the right,
wings, legs, thighs piled high in the center.
Now he looks like a wild rooster
in a country where people are starving.

His arms flap, his talons reach towards his daughter,
until he notices the attendant's
metallic spoon and its contents—
orange baby food.
He swivels his head, mesmerized,
watching the spoon
inch towards his mouth.

ONCE HE OWNED LANGUAGE

Words were as precious
as his stamp collection of countries
he never visited,
proper grammar was his creed.
Willa, it is either 'exact' or 'the same'
never 'the exact same.'

Now words disappear
in the blear of his brain,
as he tries to grab onto anyone
who comes into the hospital room.
If they get closer
he makes kissing sounds.

The doctors say it is time.
His brain, the size of a Cro-Magnon man's
is more like a fossil than a living organ,
but he is petrified of death, my father.

He who feared going for a drive without my mother
will make this journey alone.

I'm cold, I'm afraid, fat ass,
are the last three phrases
that collapse on shore,
while the others panting, struggling
to keep their heads
above water
are sucked down.

Soon it will be as if language never knew him,
and he will stare at the hands
of the clock on the wall
across from his bed,
and then...he will stop staring.

GOOD AS DEAD

tangled up in drips and tubes
                    IV bags grow on metal trees
            a machine breathes for me
    I can still think   that's something
                    Ben must be on another floor

    I cannot speak
            I'm good as dead
                    I won't be like a stroke victim
        with words stuck inside me

I refuse
                    to use a speaking gizmo
            sound like a metallic creature
        that no one understands anyway

        I'd like to punch someone
            Of course I won't
        If there's any fight left in me

            I'll write

                                words
        that scream
                        across the page

REMOVING THE INTRAVENOUS LINE

Had you already begun to die,
potassium and sodium
barely pumping into your cells,
while I walked on cobblestones
through the arched Lane of the Messiah
in Zefat's old quarter painted white and blue
against the evil eye?

Did I try to chant a *niggun,*
hear an unearthly echo in a dark corridor
above a pool of water
in the Old City's Church of St. Ann,
as you started to dehydrate
and your mouth opened
to receive ice chips?

Was I in a conference room at the King David
when I conjured your cat eyes and lips like mine,
your cells in a frenzy to stay alive?

Wish I was at the Wall
among women imbued with God's spirit,
my cheek against stone, tucking
a slip of paper into a crack
with my farewell:
Go gently, Dadzill.

ELEGY

Thank you
for making Willa with me,
walking on the outside, letting me schlep you
to Marsha's, although you hated her poor me act,
for saying I am more beautiful than Leslie Caron,
accompanying me to innumerable
clothing stores and beauty parlors,
where you waited impatiently, for pouring
us Cokes and putting out the can of Planters
while we watched T.V., closing the clasps
of my necklaces, letting me be
when I read with the light on
and you wanted sleep.

When you resorted to bringing soda bottles to pee in,
and started forgetting how to get places,
you still took me and "the ladies"
on long drives, my hearing so bad,
Marie, Minna and I sat together in the back seat
while you were the chauffeur in the front alone.

Now Brooklyn, the streets of its neighborhoods:
Brownsville – Borough Park – Crown Heights –
Red Hook – Canarsie,
that you knew as intimately as my body
are no longer yours, and the treacherous Interboro
you drove through the ghetto to get to,
although I pleaded with you to go another way,
is mourning the loss of your curses
and the insistence of your horn.

SECTION TWO

SECTION TWO

ESTHER & WILLA

ESTHER & WILLA

BEN'S FUNERAL

I make my grand entrance on a stretcher
carried by two large female attendants.
One holds my portable oxygen tank
like a football.

If I weren't so miserable
I would feel like Cleopatra
being presented to her public,
but my Ben (who knew just how to enrage me)
is dead, my hearing aids aren't worth a damn,
and I have nothing to write with.

The funeral director pins
a black ribbon, shiny, tiny
and cut in the middle
to my right lapel, to remind me
that Ben isn't sitting next to me,
and I haven't died.

At least there are handouts.
The Lord is my shepherd...
I decipher a few Hebrew letters.
My daughter talks in front of the hall,
tears stream down her face.
I can't hear a thing.
I'm too upset to have any success
reading lips. I don't care that she speaks for me.

Ben never listened to either of us anyway.
When I told him quietly at that fancy Chinese place
with the red lacquer chopsticks
that mu shu pork is bad for his cholesterol,
he yelled in front of my new son-in-law:
"Fuck-you, Esther."

I couldn't even compose the right eulogy.
Somehow my papa, who dropped dead
of a heart attack before he could collect
Social Security, was dying again,
not my Ben, my punching bag,
my ball and chain,
the man who would never leave me
until now.

GRIEF

The sorcerers are bored and frustrated
standing in their glittery robes and pointy hats
in the corner of my parents' small kitchen
where the cupboards never close properly,
the pilot light always goes out, and
my father remains spindly and mute
as before he died.

They kill time rolling small glass balls
in their palms and conjuring
the electric can opener
to delid all the tuna cans,
but finally the incantations and
wand waving work.

My father is morphing
into his debonair self, tall of carriage
as if a picture were about to be taken
in three-quarter profile, a pipe in his mouth.

He vanishes.
Ashes burn in an ashtray,
the room thick with sweet smoke.

He reappears plumper, but still translucent
holding a bowl with a puddle
of vanilla ice cream and canned peach juice.

He floats down and sits.
The index cards are still

where he left them
waiting for names of uncracked books
and Dewey decimals.

The sorcerers do my bidding
and free him to be
who he never was in life.
Today he knows origami.
Under his hands
library index cards moonlight
as snails, whales and kangaroos.

The sorcerers are delighted with themselves.
Now, in search of my mother
they squish together for a ride
in the motorized stair chair
my father used at the end.

They find her fast asleep in the den
bent over a crossword puzzle.
When she awakens
all the empty squares are filled-in with:

      I LOVE YOU I

           L
        Y O U
         V
I WILL ALWAYS LOVE YOU

LARYNGECTOMY

They cut out her voice,
like so many before
and after her.
Now others will decide they know
what she is thinking and
will speak for her.
But there will always be the yellow pad,
the spiral notebook,
the loose sheet of paper
by a bed, on an end table,
attached with a magnet to the refrigerator;
the sharpened pencil, the fine point pen,
the black magic marker hanging from a string
and the words– wise, fierce, raucous
filling up the pages of the world.

THE STOMA SPEAKS

You used to show off your willowy neck
and play with the miniature 14 carat gold apple
that dangled just above the clavicle
where I now gape.

I wish I were a disk of cookie dough
that could be pressed back into your flesh,
a knife never taken to it.

Unless you're alone,
you hide me.

How will you disown me today?

Which mock turtleneck
will be pulled over me:
the purple, the turquoise, the rust?

POST-ITS

With Esther's mother's money from the corset store they moved to Canarsie,
to a house that stood alone with a front yard and a backyard, and bought
a barbecue.

They were close enough to Jamaica Bay that seagulls circled overhead and cried.
When the wind was right Esther and Ben inhaled the sea.

Now Esther would leave Brooklyn for good, and the only home she ever owned.
Ben was nowhere. The Jewish agency had taken all his clothes and the hangers
that held them.

At least she could choose what to bring to her one bedroom apartment near her
daughter in "Oregone."

Esther stuck post-it notes to the reupholstered maroon couch, the green lamp that
looked like a cactus, the cedar box lined with red velvet that held the faux sterling
silver, the abstract acrylic by the hippie artist she met at the Greenwich Village
Art Show, who said it was painted on a trip. Only years later did she understand
he did not mean "while traveling."

Of course, she would squeeze the king-size bed into her new bedroom. Her
daughter remembers her parents at the farthest edges of that vast bed, like two
freighters separated by thick fog. But it wasn't always that way.

IN AN AIRPLANE LAVATORY
ON ROUTE TO HER NEW HOME

Forty-five minutes and the OCCUPIED
sign is still on. Passengers are kicking
the door and yelling *are you taking a bath?*

At least she doesn't hear them.
She is concentrating.
Her tiny hearing aids hidden by her hair
are no more functional than cowrie shells.
She is not disabled… others are.
She mouths *nebekh,* shaking her head
when she sees a blind man with a seeing eye dog,
or watches a teenager in an electric wheelchair,
although "she walks so slowly
she could be standing still,"
a phrase my father muttered
as he slowed down for her to catch up.

In these cramped quarters she is all efficiency.
She sits on the closed toilet bowl,
Millie's lacquerware tray and the mortar
on her lap. She mashes her pills with the pestle.
I am allowed to fill a plastic cup with water,
snap the tab off a can of liquid nutrition.
She smiles as she unfurls the peg tube
jutting from her belly, and deftly crowns it
with her funnel and pours.

All items are dried and stashed away
in a Meier & Frank shopping bag.
We emerge normal as everyone else
buckled-up in their seats, who like us
later, or sooner, will die.

ON A GOOD MORNING

I look in the mirror
and don't have to use plastic tweezers
to pull gunk out of my stoma.

I haven't misplaced the screwdriver
to twist off the tab on a can of Compleat Modified,
so I won't starve to death,

my incontinence pad is dry,
the *Oregonian* is on the mat outside my door,

I'm not angry about cancer taking my voice,
(no one has to talk out loud when they are alone anyway),

Accupril, Capoten, Lopressor, Synthroid,
the pills I wish I could live without,
are in alphabetical order,

my arm doesn't ache
holding the feeding tube and funnel up high
like the Statue of Liberty, to pull
the slowpoke coffee-colored liquid
and the ground-up pills into my stomach,

the poorly translated closed-captions
on my T.V. screen almost make sense,

and I'm able to work that damn MailStation
to read an e-mail from my daughter who writes:
Ma, you have to learn to use it.
It's your voice now!

HER LIFE AS A READER

Words enter her stealthily,
join hands to become sentences,
skip into story:

All the characters tell her
their secrets– that they were once young
and used to sit in a window seat
in the house of the book's parlour.

They would only leave when they had to
go to school, play with their sisters, or have fun
the way they were supposed to by jumping
double-dutch or constructing a worm farm.

Years later, in those rare moments of quiescence
after putting the children down,
the characters would climb into the fifth storey
of the gingerbread mansion
appearing on the hill.

Sometimes they would lift their hands up high
and catch paragraphs from *Orlando* or
Look Homeward Angel, and only the smell
of apple pie would entice them
to vacate the premises.

For some, the delicious is now forbidden
and those pages tell the tale of a woman
who only speaks through writing
in a spiral notebook.

She still loves to prop up in bed,
a lamp clipped to her bedpost,
a book open in her lap.
Hers may be the only light
in their home, in their town.

ESTHER SCHNEBERG VISITS ABBA KOVNER AT SLOAN-KETTERING

Israeli poet and resistance fighter Abba Kovner died in 1987 of throat cancer.

She walks towards him clutching a thick notebook
with a black marbleized cover.
There is no need for introductions.
He knows she is a landsman
from the shtetl of speechlessness.

His bed is cranked-up,
behind his head, a pillow.
He motions her to pull up a chair.

She opens her notebook, passes it to him.
He scribbles in pen,
                    How long?

She leans towards him
to retrieve the book.
Now she writes
in the volley of conversation
between blue lines:
"Nine months."

                    I think a week. The drugs keep me fuzzy.
                    Being in the underground was easier.

She snatches the book back.
"You escaped through sewers,
slept in forests.
You wouldn't go to the slaughter."

                    I'm not brave.

I was 22.
Maybe I've said all I need to say.

"As a child, I was exiled to the listeners group,
not to sing. I never suffered, not really, until this.
Even giving birth to my daughter,
who I want you to know is a poet,
I was sedated."

I could deliver a funny line,
but my timing was always off.
You have to tell a good joke,
written down isn't amusing.

"I can't eat by mouth anymore,
live on liquid nutrition,
a feeding tube protrudes."

I'd like honey on my tongue.

"Although I've lost my sense of smell
I still know what's rotten."

I don't think of myself as religious.
I want to speak two words, just two:
Yitgadal viyitkadash

"I want to shriek—
my rage the night train's loudest whistle."

Stars don't go out when we die.

"Now you're talking."

PIERCING ONE EAR

That self-important *momzer,*
the Portland nose and throat man
with the porcelain Chinese urns.
Where does he think he is, on Park Avenue?
He thought he could show up
the New York doctors
and let me dine again. At Bishop Morris,
I too would hold a glass of water
to my lips and swallow
just like the other *alte kakers.*

He sent me for a CAT Scan
and got my hopes up.

I was always a sucker
for suspension bridges—
how their sides raise up to the sky
and seamlessly remerge,
but the bridge between the pharynx
and my gullet has been blown-up.

No Army Corps of Engineers
will come to the rescue.
Food can't leap from one side
to the other. Perhaps Dr. Botox
thought he could string a hammock.

For my consolation prize
the great man re-pierced my left ear.
It closed up from all the aggravation.

I appreciate symmetry. With two holes
I can wear earrings again.
Tomorrow I'll model
the blue-green stone ones
my daughter brought from Jerusalem.

ALTERATIONS

The woman putting plastic over finished garments hears the buzzer. Two grey-haired women walk in, one middle-aged, one very old and unsteady, as if she's wearing high heels for the first time and skinny, like a body wrung out of its insides.

The old lady writes in a notebook. The one who must be her daughter reads out loud what she wants.

The old lady must have brought all the trousers in her closet. The woman sees her as a balloon losing air, a moon waning, and she knows that taking up hems or moving over clasps won't stop the old lady shrinking to nothing.

PHONE CALLS, 3 AM

I

The Mother

I must call...
Maybe it can wait until morning.
Did we agree:
two rings or four,
then hang up?

I don't want to bother them
in the middle of the night,

but when I went to the bathroom
the front of my nightgown
was drenched in blood. It oozes
from the corroded skin
around my peg tube.

I tape down gauze bandages.
They swell with blood.

Two rings or four?
I'll stay on the phone.
She'll know it's me.
My breath will insist.

II

The Daughter

Hello...?
Only breathing.
I hang-up.

The phone rings again.

We hope it's a wrong number—
an adolescent calling back his girlfriend
who just slammed down the phone,
a pervert's exhalation,
his heavy breathing
before climax,

but I know that cry hidden
inside frantic breath,
the husky voice
that doubled for Lauren Bacall's.

Ma, don't worry we're on our way.

BIN LADEN'S BODY

I watch the towers collapse
over and over again,
and can do nothing
but grieve for the City
that brought everyone
from everywhere to me.

Although I'm not there,
soot sticks to my bathrobe
and uncombed hair.

I can barely breathe,
as I hold myself, and rock
on my La-Z-Boy
shipped from Brooklyn.
I couldn't get dressed today.

My eyes ache from smoke.
White-grey ash clings to me.
Tiny pieces of steel and concrete powder
coat the inside of my windows,
my pill bottles, my throw pillows,
my eyeglasses, between my fingers,
and the pen I write with.

I hand my daughter my pad:
My wish is,
like my body,
Bin Laden's should betray him
bit by bit.

HOW COULD YOU?

The journey's over. Love to all.
                        Carolyn G. Heilbrun

How could you hoard pills, and put a plastic bag over your head? Nothing was wrong with you. You were going to live each day. Your life was an idyll, reading with your feet up in your apt. on Central Park West, while I who would have killed to move to Manhattan, never left Brooklyn.

I too hate the drudgery of airports, the claustrophobia of flying, the ordeal of shopping and entertaining. I bet you never learned to drive either. We were certain our husbands would outlive us. Only one of us was correct. We both fiercely loved our daughters, transplants to Oregon, and would like them even if they weren't ours.

After retirement, I hoped to write the great American novel, scribbled a few things, nostalgia about my grandmothers, but if I were really a wordsmith like you and my daughter, I wouldn't write only for assignments.

You quit, while I, mute, with teeth and nothing to bite, am not ready to face how immediately after you go, the world seals over.

HUNGER STRIKE

I can almost understand why
that Japanese cult
released sarin in subways,
and the people who hate America
filled envelopes with anthrax.

I couldn't write loud enough,
red enough,

> No nursing home! No chemo!
> No surgery!!

turn the pen into a poker.

I never could throw a punch,
but when I could still yell,
you'd be afraid.
I tore into the yellow lined pages,
but my pellets of anger were wadded paper.
Nobody was listening, not the doctors,
not you...

My gurgling, empty stomach became a sonic boom.
It shook-up the doctors who think they know everything.

Darling, I can accept that the prednisone
made me a little paranoid; I thought
you were in league with them
and were using your power of attorney
to send me to corridors packed with the palsied.

Your aunt Marsha was the only one in our family
more stubborn than me. Like Bobby Sands,
I am willing to starve for what I believe. He died,
but in two days I was back in my apartment. The hospital
even supplied a special vehicle to take me home.

I couldn't understand why someone
who threw her mother away
would be crying, when I shoved
the brown paper bag at you containing
my can opener, funnel, and
Compleat Modified,
as if to say: *Here, you drink it!*

MY HAIR

I could get a wig
and look like Orthodox Jewish women
who think they are so glamorous
wearing someone else's hair.
If God really wanted women to cover their heads,
so men wouldn't lose control,
he'd command them
to tuck their wayward strands
under a simple kerchief,
not beneath an expensive *sheitel*
to make you look like Farah Fawcett.

I thought the whole idea was modesty.
I know I still have good legs, but at eighty,
with or without hair on my head
not many men, except your father,
would get excited seeing me
creep down the street.

Bald from chemo,
I would gain a few months,
perhaps a year.
I prefer to die with hair.

Weds. Oct. 10, 2001

<u>TO BE READ CAREFULLY</u>

My Dearest Children – Willa & Robin,

It finally occurred to me! You've known for some time that I am terminal

and were right to recommend Hospice. Now that I understand that

I cannot be cured, I welcome Hospice too. We can operate together at last.

My only question is <u>why</u> all the <u>meds</u>? Also, I want my Hospice here.

The morphine pad is very welcome, but I think it should be applied to the rump

and can be changed 3 (?) days by my caretaker.

I hope the meds are still in alphabetical order on the desk. Also

I can't find my writing book. I like the style of the book, but it is

too heavy. Get me the same book, but half the thickness. I look

forward to seeing you as often as I can, and also to death, whenever it comes.

I can take nutrition as before, but I need a steady hand, not mine.

I am sorry I gave you a bad time.

All My Love,
Esther

HOSPICE

Esther smelled like rotten eggs.
From her stoma a low wheezing sound.
The skin around her feeding tube was raw and pussy.

No chatter, cancer took her voice box.

She agreed to morphine,
let the nurse rub it directly on her gums.

She couldn't eliminate,
skipped some nutrition times,
complained of nausea.

Her daughter is a poet with a book.
I saw it by her bedside.

Esther's handwriting became harder and
harder to decipher. She pointed to this
in her notebook: *I'm Jewish.*
         There is no God.

I hoped the job would last a few weeks.
I hate calling families after 1AM.

Her eyes grew wide,
her face soft and silky.
I wrapped her in the afghan she crocheted
and named *The Mondrian.*

RENDING THE GARMENT

In Jewish ritual clothes are torn in mourning.

The night before my mother goes into the ground
I try to eat
in my hotel near Kennedy,
but since Sept. 11th
the restaurant is temporarily closed.

In the still open souvenir shop
I find a t-shirt that fits me.
A youth M preshrunk 10-12,
an I ♥ N Y t-shirt.

I go up to my room.
On the wall above my bed is a print
of a colonial lower Manhattan
and outside my window
is bumper to bumper traffic.

My mother is a photograph,
a hoarse voice on the answering machine,
an afghan of primary-colored squares
girded with black wool,
a small coleus with pink-spotted leaves
outside apt. 306,
a man in the street with a hole in his throat,
a silver ring with a moonstone
on my index finger.

I pull the t-shirt over my head,
claw at the red heart,
but the fabric won't rip.

I'm forced to use the small blade
on my nail clipper to make a slit.
Now my hands can tear the heart
that hides the one that beats.

SECTION THREE

SECTION THREE

WILLA

WILLA

THE FINAL PLOY

Your parents' final ploy
was purchasing you a grave plot
in the cemetery on Long Island.
You were supposed to lie between your aunt
and your father, who never got along.

Since you won't be there to shush them,
they can bicker forever.

BEN'S SHOES

Bharata put Rama's sandals on Ayodhya's red and gold throne.
The shoes remain silent if well pleased.

Ramayana

It seemed like he had hundreds
living in shoe trees,
but the pair she liked the best were dressy,
black and smooth as skin.
When she was little, he wore them with a tuxedo
and cummerbund, his hair slicked back.
She was sure he was dancing with princesses.

Later she understood he was only the hired help,
and that he stood in many kitchens
with others similarly attired
waiting to make an entrance,
holding high above their heads silver trays
ablaze with cherries jubilee.

After she left home
he hung up his cummerbund,
had trouble bending over,
carried a shoe horn in his pocket,
and still polished his black shoes
for the weddings of other people's daughters.

Now she keeps the pair unceremoniously
in a corner of the broom closet,
and like Rama's sandals, her father's shoes
are regal with disdain.

They knock against each other
whenever she utters a double negative,
forgets to turn off the bathroom light
or leaves her shoes in the middle of the floor.

ODE TO ROTHKO

I call him the last rabbi of Western Art.
                              Stanley Kunitz

When you were nine, you stopped
saying Kaddish for your father
every morning as prescribed
at Ahavai Sholom in Portland
and never returned to pray,
but inside your *shul*
the *Shabbos* bride opens herself
and the Red Sea parts.

Now I live in that "dull and provincial
house of the dead,"
you couldn't wait to leave,
where we both sought the West Hills
deep in winter, to face
Mount Hood, Mount St. Helens,
and a sliver of Mount Adams
hiding in the night sky.

Marcus Rothkowitz,
when we were still living in New York,
and you were already old,
did I walk past you
as you left your 57th Street gallery
to flee to your studio on East 69th?

For hours or days you would *daven*,
your whole body a paintbrush.
Glowing layers of mauve-violet twilight
would envelope you,
three smudged-edged rectangles
would transport you to the *Ayn Sof*
where joy is sorrow,
sorrow, joy.

BICYCLING IN BELIZE

Two shiny bikes are waiting
on the porch for tomorrow's excursion.
She is afraid
of the simple machine.

He plucks a fragrant plumeria
blossom and tucks it behind her ear.
He promises he will hold onto the bike,
won't let her fall.

She remembers a pink tricycle,
fluttering plastic strips,
her little legs pumping.

Soon she is peddling along a mud-packed road.
There is room for everyone—
trucks, golf carts, bicycles,
and this tourist
who is gliding by
ringing her tiny bell.

WILLA'S HAIRS

After my sweatshirt comes out of the dryer
I find one on the sleeve.
Driving home from the mountains
one has attached to my ski pants.
When we awaken in the morning
one clings to my chest.
I wonder... after she is gone,
could my green-eyed one be made again
from a single long white hair.

FIFTY-TWO

My exotic look is wearing thin. No longer white hair
with a young face, bangs now hide the lines
on my forehead. My arms have white dots
where the pigment was. Scratches of blue invade my legs
and no longer supple ankles. I am still thinner than most
women, but now tights are too tight and leave the imprint
of their seams down my middle. My behind jiggles, and
I wear panty liners against whatever might ooze out,

but my small breasts remain pertish, my cheeks smooth.
When we lie in bed, and you press your cheek to mine,
we are out of time, neither old, nor young—
bodies without bodies.

NOTES

Not My Type: (Yiddish) *Mittendrinen:* All of a sudden, right in the middle of everything.

My Two Grandmothers; **Ben Calls His Daughter From A Hospital In Brooklyn**; **My Hair:** (Yiddish) *Sheitel*: Wig.

Live Incubator Baby Only 25 Cents!: Dr. Martin Couney was called the "Incubator Doctor." From 1903-1945, his premature babies were a sideshow attraction at Coney Island.

Ben Schneberg Meets Jacob Lawrence At Hillside Hospital: "Oyfn Pripetchik"is a well known Yiddish song written by Mark Warszawsky.

Eagelton, I Know How You Feel; Piercing One Ear: (Yiddish) *Momzer:* Bastard.

Someone I Don't Know Is Being Murdered: (Khmer) *Riels:* Cambodian currency; (DESs) District Electoral Supervisors for (UNTAC) the United Nations Transitional Authority in Cambodia, were responsible for setting up registration sites and educating registrars during the first "free and fair" election since the time of the French colonial period; (NADK) National Army of Democratic Kampuchea, (CPAF) Cambodian People's Armed Forces.

Teaching Poetry At The Postgraduate Center For Mental Health: The epigraph is from Anne Sexton's unpublished poem "Out at the Mental Hospital" about McLean's.

Willa's Kapparot: In some traditional Jewish communities the ceremony of Kapparot is performed at dawn on the day before Yom Kippur. A woman takes a hen in her left hand, lays her right hand on its head and swings it three times above her head saying, "This is my substitute, this is my exchange, this is my atonement. This fowl will go to death and I will enter upon a good, long life and peace."

Removing The Intravenous Line: (Hebrew) *Niggun*: A wordless song, often a lament.

In An Airplane Lavatory On Route To Her New Home: (Yiddish) *Nebekh*: An unlucky, pitiable person.

Esther Schneberg Visits Abba Kovner At Sloan-Kettering: (Hebrew) *Yitgadal viyitkadash*: First two words of the Jewish prayer for the dead, "*...stars don't go out when we die.*" is from "Detached Verses," *Sloan – Kettering,* by Abba Kovner (Schocken Books, 2002)

Piercing One Ear: (Yiddish) *Alte kakers*: Old people, literally means "old shitters."

How Could You?: Feminist scholar Carolyn G. Heilbrun committed suicide on Oct. 9, 2003.

Ode To Rothko: (Hebrew) *Ayn Sof*: Refers to the infinite, boundless, without end, all attributes of the Divine.

ABOUT THE AUTHOR

Willa Schneberg has authored four other poetry collections: *In The Margins of The World* (Plain View Press), recipient of the Oregon Book Award in Poetry, *Box Poems* (Alice James Books), *Storytelling In Cambodia* (Calyx Books), and the letterpress chapbook *The Books of Esther* (Paper Crane Press) produced in conjunction with her interdisciplinary exhibit at the Oregon Jewish Museum, Fall of 2012.

Willa has read at the Library of Congress, her poems were heard on Garrison Keillor's The Writer's Almanac, and she has been a fellow at Yaddo and MacDowell. She is a social worker in private practice and a visual artist. Willa lives with her husband in Portland, Oregon.

www.threewayconversation.org.

MUDFISH INDIVIDUAL POET SERIES

Box Turtle Press/Attitude Art Inc.
184 Franklin Street
New York, New York 10013